Original title:
Buttons of Destiny

Copyright © 2025 Creative Arts Management OÜ
All rights reserved.

Author: Amelia Montgomery
ISBN HARDBACK: 978-1-80586-006-8
ISBN PAPERBACK: 978-1-80586-478-3

The Trajectory of Touch

A poke to the left, a swipe on the right,
It's a dance of the fingers, what a sight!
With a tap and a twist, the moment is near,
Who knew digital chaos could bring us such cheer!

Missed calls and bad texts, oh what a thrill,
Accidental selfies that give us a chill.
We navigate fate with just one little press,
In this pixelated world, we're all in a mess!

The Ferrule of the Future

In a world of gadgets that beep and that boop,
We're all trying to make sense of this loop.
A flick and a flicker, what could go wrong?
Oh look, now I'm singing a phone's silly song!

They say this device can change how we live,
But the only gift it brings is a funny quip.
Oh, the struggle is real, with each pocket surprise,
It's either drowned out laughter or screens in our eyes!

The Toggle of Trust

When toggles are flipped, the truth must be sought,
A switch to the right, yet chaos is wrought.
"Just one more click!" I happily insist,
Now I'm caught in a loop I surely missed!

Trust is a button all too easily pressed,
With promises made and then tossed on the jest.
In this whimsical realm, who's fooling who now?
We're all just a click away with a laugh and a bow!

Grips of Grasping

With a grip on our phones and a swipe to the fame,
We juggle our lives in this ridiculous game.
A slip of the thumb sends us running around,
In search of solutions yet never quite found!

The grips that we hold are both tight and absurd,
Oh, the tales of mishaps, you've surely heard.
On this wild ride of fate and of fun,
Let's cheer for the blunders we've all accidentally done!

Emblems of the Unknown

In a drawer of fate, I found my socks,
Tangled mess of knots and silly blocks.
A matchmaker's dream of colors so bright,
But where's the pair? It's quite a delight!

Lost in laughter, I search them all,
One's hiding here, the other's on call.
They're plotting mischief, 'Oh, look, a shoe!'
This game of hide-and-seek—who knew?

A Tangle of Paths

A road map unfolds with a wink and a grin,
One route leads to cake, another to sin.
Twists and turns that tickle my fate,
Every choice made is a twist of the plate!

I stumble upon paths that never align,
One's paved with jelly, the other's with wine.
Do I venture forth with my jester's hat?
Here's hoping I find a good scallywag spat!

The Closure of Possibility

A door creaks open, then flaps in the breeze,
I find it amusing, does it aim to please?
Knobs jingle with laughter beneath my hand,
It's joy in absurdity that I understand.

I peek through the crack, see a parade of clowns,
Waving their arms, wearing mismatched crowns.
A realm where socks dance and giggles ignite,
I decide to join in! Oh what a sight!

Fabricated Futures

In the cupboard of hopes, I concoct a plan,
To create a new world with a spatula and pan.
Stirring up dreams like a chef's wild delight,
Each whim added sparks a new laugh in the night.

Yet in my vision, spaghetti joins cheese,
A wacky invention that brings me to knees.
With marshmallow clouds all around the sun,
I herd this chaos—oh, what silly fun!

The Tapestry of Choices

In a world where choices bloom,
Like daisies in a room,
Do I wear the polka dots,
Or the stripes that tie in knots?

Each stitch a quirky tale,
Of socks that flop and fail,
I ponder which to select,
As my fashion saves or wrecks!

Twists of Fortune

I trip on decisions wide,
With luck as my goofy guide,
Should I chase the flying pie,
Or just watch it zooming by?

Every turn's a wild dance,
Like a cat in a silly trance,
With fortunes that twist and bend,
And laughter that never ends!

Fastened Futures

My future's a jigsaw mix,
Of weird and wacky tricks,
Shall I bloom in plaid today,
Or find a polka-dot ballet?

With zippers and buttons bright,
My choices take to flight,
I fasten dreams absurd,
And hope for the awfully heard!

The Clasp of Whimsy

A twist here and a flip there,
Life's like a clown with flair,
Should I hop on a rubber boot,
Or dance with a funky fruit?

With giggles sewn in seams,
And laughter spilling dreams,
Whimsy clasps me tight,
In a world of pure delight!

Twine of Transformation

In a world where fortunes twist and twine,
A pickle jar became my life's design.
I pressed a button, saw a cat in a hat,
Danced with a cactus, and oh, how he sat!

A squirrel in a tuxedo twirled and whirled,
While leaving behind a mess that unfurled.
I hopped on a trampoline made of cheese,
And floated through dreams with the greatest of ease.

Each leap brought a giggle, a twist of my fate,
Burping out rainbows, how can this be fate?
The clock struck twelve, and the cheese turned to dust,
But I laughed with the squirrel, in fun we trust!

So here's to the twine, with its comical flair,
Every twist and turn filled with whimsy and care.
In laughter we find our true colors shine,
In a world ever-changing, we're all intertwined.

The Knot of Knowledge

I tied my shoes with a string of bright lore,
And learned that wisdom comes from every door.
I asked a goldfish for a sage's advice,
He winked and replied, 'Have you tried sushi rice?'

A selfie with a cactus? That's simply divine!
I posted on socials, 'This cactus is mine!'
The likes started pouring like rain from the sky,
As I giggled and snorted, oh me, oh my!

The universe chuckled at my silly stunt,
A dance with a llama? A wild, crazy hunt!
I spun him around, with my hat flying high,
Together we soared, like a kite in the sky.

In knots of confusion, I found a great laugh,
Knowledge is best when it's served with a gaff.
So I'll juggle my lessons, let whimsy unfold,
With laughter and knots, let the fun stories be told!

The Fastening of Dreams

In a land where dreams get stuck,
Sewing kits, oh what luck!
With threads of thought, we twist and tie,
Hoping our wishes will soar and fly.

A needle's dance, a jolly jig,
Patching together hopes—oh so big!
But sometimes they snag, those pesky seams,
Leaving us tangled in wild dreams.

Laughter echoes as we stitch away,
Creating outfits for our sunny day.
With silly patterns, bright and bold,
We wear our hopes like tales retold.

In a world of fabric, wild and vast,
We find our joy in each stitch cast.
So gather round, it's time to play,
Fashion our futures in a fun-filled way.

The Pull of Purpose

With every tug, we take a chance,
Each little pull begins a dance.
Goals in hand, we giggle and grin,
Off we go, let the fun begin!

A rubber band, stretched oh so wide,
What will happen if we take a ride?
With every pull, a new delight,
Chasing dreams through day and night.

Like a yo-yo, we bounce back fast,
Learning lessons from our past.
The silly missteps turn us wise,
From every quirky twist we rise.

So let us pull, let not fear bind,
Embrace the whims, be light of mind.
In this playful game of love and glee,
We weave our dreams, you and me!

The Zipper of Zest

A zipper's zip, a joyful sound,
With every slide, excitement's found.
Clothes and thoughts, we fasten tight,
Harnessing fun—what a silly sight!

Up and down, we glide and glide,
Zest in our steps, let's enjoy the ride.
With laughter rising like a kite,
Together we zip, holding dreams so bright.

In the closet of life, we find our flair,
Mixing patterns, colors everywhere.
The zaniest looks make us chuckle loud,
Standing out, we're oh so proud!

So zip it up, and off we go,
Into the world, putting on a show.
With hearts so light, and spirits bold,
Every zip's a story waiting to be told.

Connections in Threads

Each thread a tale, weaving around,
Connections made without a sound.
We stitch our friends into one whole,
Creating laughter—mind and soul.

Tangled knots and loops so fun,
Sewing together 'til the day is done.
With every laugh, a stitch will hold,
Our tapestry shines with stories bold.

In this fabric of life we share,
Every thread's a memory we care.
Colors clash, but oh what joy,
In this quirky quilt, there's no decoy.

So gather your threads, let's unite,
With colors and patterns, all so bright.
In this patchwork world, we'll stand and cheer,
For every connection brings us near!

Sewn Secrets

In a world of threads and seams,
Mysteries stitch together dreams.
With every tug and playful pull,
Life's little quirks become quite full.

Bobbins dance, a cheeky show,
Winking at us from below.
Who knew a pocket could hold such glee?
A lost sock's journey—what could it be?

From pockets deep, secrets emerge,
In patches worn, fates converge.
The hemline laughs, it knows the score,
Sending surprises through every door.

The Fabric of Chance

Woven tightly, tangled thread,
Life's a quilt; never misled.
Patches of luck, a silly spree,
Who'd think it's all so fancy-free?

A seamstress smiles, with twinkle in eye,
As patterns swirl and twirl up high.
Unruly ruffles, a raucous cheer,
Hoping for stitches that won't disappear!

Each misstep makes a tale to tell,
Stitch by stitch, we craft our spell.
Silly mistakes, like fabric spritz,
Turn all our woes into comic bits.

Tactile Traces

Through fingertips, sensations roam,
Each textile whispers, 'Welcome home!'
Silks that shimmer, wool that shags,
Bring forth tales of all our jags.

Velvet hugs that make us grin,
Joys and jests wrapped up within.
Cotton cakes, how sweet they seem,
Life's fabric is a patchwork dream!

Swatches tell of accidents bright,
A coffee stain? Oh what a sight!
Each texture jests, with playful tease,
In life's grand weave, we find our ease.

Fasten Your Fate

With a click and a clack, fate's on display,
Fasten up now, come what may!
Snaps and zippers, oh what a mix,
Life's opening up, toss in the tricks!

Giggling threads, the needle's dance,
In every twist, there's more to prance.
Unruly threads, like jokes they fly,
Who thought a cuff could tickle the sky?

With every loop, we sway and leap,
Our stitches sing, our secrets keep.
So gather 'round, it's time to play,
Fasten your fates — let's seize the day!

Binds of Bewilderment

In a drawer, odd trinkets lie,
Each with a story, oh my, oh my!
A shiny one sings, a rusty one squeaks,
Together they dance, and giggle in weeks.

A popping noise comes from a red sphere,
It jumps up high, oh dear, oh dear!
Gravity's friend? Not quite, I guess,
Just a drama queen in an old dress.

Six pairs of eyes stare at a cat,
What's she thinking? I think she's fat!
With buttons for eyes, she stares right back,
Time for a chase, or a nap attack.

And so we laugh at this treasure chest,
Where things get tangled and never rest.
In each little find, a memory stirs,
Life's a jigsaw, wrapped in purrs.

Loops of Longing

A hula hoop spins with a giggle and cheer,
Round and round until it's near.
Fall down, get up, what's the score?
Life is a loop, but who keeps the door?

In my socks I've found a note,
"The universe works; just stay afloat!"
But left foot in right, I still trip and flip,
Gravity chuckles at my funny flip.

When strings get tangled in a mess of knots,
The cat curls up, or so it plots.
A chase ensues, at the bottom I land,
Only to find, she's stolen my hand!

But delight, it seems, is found within,
For in every flop, there's a cheeky grin.
So I roll with the loops, and skip with the bounce,
Turning life's folly into a joyous flounce!

The Closure of Chance

A door creaks open, a treasure lies,
A quirky contraption, oh what a surprise!
But which way to turn? The handle's stuck,
I twist, I pull, and then—oh, what luck!

A dragon pops out from a box of toys,
With a trumpet of war and a bag full of noise!
"Let's dance on the ceiling!" it roars with glee,
While friends hold their sides, "Is it you or me?"

Yet chance is a jester, a playful tease,
It pings like a ball in a game of freeze.
With every mishap, I'm pulled into fate,
Tell me a joke, I can hardly wait!

So here we sit, in life's silly play,
With unexpected laughs lighting the way.
Through closures and chances we bounce and grin,
In this grand adventure, let's dive right in!

Alignments of Ambition

A line of ants marches, oh so proud,
With a crumb on the move, they gather a crowd.
But which way to go? Confusion sets in,
They rally in circles, where's the win-win?

An archer aims high for more than just fun,
His arrows go flying, but only one's won.
Stuck in a tree, a bird holds the prize,
"Here's your ambition!" it chirps with surprise.

In pursuit of big dreams, the squirrel does leap,
Straight into trouble, or maybe a heap.
Yet with every misstep and every near fall,
He twirls and he twirls—he's now in a ball!

So here we combine ambition and zest,
With laughter and joy, we'll conquer the quest.
In this vibrant tale, our spirits will soar,
With goofy pursuits, who could ask for more?

Veils of Variable Futures

In the drawer of chance we sift,
Finding treasures and some junk too,
A sock that's lonely, old and stiff,
We're here for laughs, not much ado.

With every flick of fate's great hand,
A whirl of odds begins to dance,
The cat's old toy, a rubber band,
And who knew socks could lead to romance?

A sneeze reveals a path unclear,
A spill on cake, a frosted fate,
A hiccup causes cheer to veer,
Are we too late or just on plate?

So chuckle as the mishaps roll,
For life's a jest with twists galore,
Embrace the chaos, that's the goal,
With each new turn, we crave for more.

The Network of Nuance

A web of giggles we construct,
With every choice, a cause and chance,
A hiccup leads to fun being plucked,
And laughter's just a funny dance.

Our plans might wobble, slip and slide,
Yet joy is found in teeter-totter,
With every guffaw, we take it in stride,
Like spilled milk humor, all things flatter.

An email sent to the wrong crew,
A mix-up with the office cake,
We navigate the zany too,
Each slip a story we can make.

So let's embrace the texts gone wrong,
The misspelled notes and jokes we share,
For in this network, we belong,
A patchwork quilt of laughter rare.

The Fold of Fate

In the paper of life we find our creases,
Doodled paths that zig and zag,
Fates may fold in funny pieces,
With every wrinkle, a laughter rag.

A skit of stumbles, dance of winks,
With mishaps lining up like ants,
A cereal spill leads to new links,
Who knew fate wore polka dot pants?

From blender whirs to puppy sighs,
The fabric holds our quirks and quirks,
In every crease, a silly surprise,
Life's just a tapestry of smirks.

So fold your tales with raucous cheer,
With clumsy joy, we'll stitch and seam,
Together we'll weave bright futures near,
In this wild and tangled dream.

Currents of Choice

On the river where decisions flow,
A boat made of whims and jests,
With paddles of laughter, here we go,
Navigating joy with playful quests.

Each twist and turn brings silly sights,
A fish that dances, a hat that flies,
With every oar, the fun ignites,
Choices like gaggles of fireflies.

The map is drawn in doodle ink,
A treasure marked with giggles bold,
Let's tip the boat, embrace the wink,
In waters where the jesters scold.

So sail away, let futures blend,
With capers that twirk and turn,
Each ripple fuels the laughter trend,
Through currents where the wild things churn.

The Link of Longing

I searched for a button, all shiny and bright,
Yet found a small dog, chasing its tail in delight.
The button I wanted was lost in the crowd,
But a giggling cat made me laugh out loud.

A friend said, 'Just look where the lost things stay!'
So we wandered in circles, hip hip hooray!
A squirrel stole my hopes, with a wink and a hop,
In this quest for a button, I just couldn't stop.

We laughed at the chaos, the buttons that fled,
And soon we were searching for ice cream instead.
With spoons like mini shovels, we dug in with glee,
Guess finding that button was sweet irony!

Webs of Wonder

Spiders were spinning, with charms like no other,
But all I could find was a sticky old brother.
He draped me in webs, said, 'Isn't this neat?'
But I wanted a button, my quest incomplete!

Dancing with mischief, a rabbit bounced by,
He wore odd socks, oh me, oh my!
He offered me carrots, a very bad trade,
For a button's true worth, who knows where it strayed?

We twirled through the grass, in this tangle of fun,
While hunters sought treasures, we'd just begun.
A treasure of laughter, a find I can see,
In the webs of this wonder, both you and me!

Lacing the Unseen

In a world of misfits, I found quite a crew,
With shoelaces tangled, we didn't know what to do.
A whispering breeze sang, 'Let's chase the unknown,'
And off we went, hearts lighter than stone.

I stumbled upon laughter that tied us in knots,
While attempting to dance amidst all the spots.
Laces became wings, or so we all thought,
As we flailed and we slipped, laughter can't be bought!

In the riddle of moments, unseen tied with joy,
We played silly games, like a juvenile ploy.
And when I tripped over, my dreams took to flight,
Celebrating the unseen until the fall of night!

The Mesh of Moments

Life's a silly mesh, knitted just for the brave,
With moments like bubbles that only misbehave.
I chased a loose thread, thinking it was grand,
But it led me to tumble right into a band!

We danced like wild wombats under a full moon,
While my socks paired with laughter, a colorful tune.
A sandwich made of jelly, a pickle on top,
In this mesh of sharp moments, we never could stop!

With twinkling eyes, we wove tales of our fate,
Creating a mesh that no one could rate.
So here's to the laughter, the moments we weave,
In this hilarious dance, there's more to believe!

Pathways of Possibility

In a land where socks go missing,
And shoes sing songs at night,
There's a road paved with gumdrops,
Where dreams take silly flight.

With squirrels wearing sunglasses,
And hats made from candy canes,
You'll laugh till your sides are sore,
As you dance in jelly rains.

Balloons float by with laughter,
Inviting all to join the fun,
You can twirl with giant marshmallows,
Till the day is finally done.

So skip along this bright pathway,
Where each step is gleeful glee,
For who knows what you'll discover,
In a world so wild and free!

The Webbing of Wishful Thinking

In a land where chairs are bouncy,
And rainbows taste like pie,
A spider spins her wishes,
Kite-flying in the sky.

Her web, a map of giggles,
With hopes that stick like glue,
Each thread a joke waiting,
To brighten up your view.

With candy crows that caw in rhymes,
And jelly beans that dance,
Every bit of whimsy here,
Makes you want to prance!

So come and catch a silly dream,
In this woven, wacky scene,
For in this joyful, crazy place,
Nothing's ever quite what it seems!

The Canvas of Chance

On a canvas stretched across the stars,
Where paint splatters with a laugh,
Each stroke reveals a funny fate,
With unicorns on a raft.

A brush dipped in giggles,
Creates suns with silly grins,
While clouds of whipped cream float by,
As the moon plays games and spins.

Each splash tells a story,
Of things that didn't quite go right,
Like painting lava lamps at noon,
Or running from a kite.

So pull on your paint-stained overalls,
And dip into this spree,
For on this canvas of life,
You'll find joy and mystery!

Threads of the Unpredictable

In a land where pants speak loudly,
And hats perform a show,
The threads that weave our fortunes,
Twist and twirl to and fro.

A shoelace greets a button,
In a dance that's quite absurd,
While threads of fate get tangled up,
In conversations unheard.

A wardrobe filled with giggles,
Winks at the socks on the floor,
And every turn of fabric here,
Opens up a brand new door.

So tug on those cosmic threads,
With a smile and a nod,
For in the dance of the unpredictable,
Life's a whimsical facade!

The Ties That Bind Us

In the drawer, they dance around,
A motley crew without a sound.
One's too big, another too small,
Yet, they gather for the grand ball.

They argue often, a silly sight,
Who will hold the pants up tight?
The lapel pins all roll their eyes,
As the floppy bow ties tell their lies.

Oh, the threadbare ones have tales to tell,
Of awkward encounters where they fell.
A strap, a clasp, a friendship formed,
In a world of fashion, they're all transformed.

So let's celebrate each quirky seam,
For who would've thought they'd form a team?
The little fasteners hold us close,
In this fabric of life, we love the most.

Mysteries in Buttonholes

In the coat, a mystery brews,
With buttonholes, one can't refuse.
Some are lost, while others fit,
In the chaos, can you make sense of it?

Oh, the shenanigans they conspire,
Each hole telling tales of mischief and fire.
One hides secrets, another's a trick,
In a world of fabrics, it's quite the pick.

Ladies and gents, come gather near,
As buttons whisper, "We're full of cheer!"
A tale of a coat that went out to dine,
And came back sporting a duck on a line.

In the realm of seams, life has its quirks,
Each buttonhole has its perks.
So let's embrace our stitched-up fate,
With laughter and joy, it's never too late.

Small Fastenings, Big Dreams

Tiny fastenings with big ideas,
They connect the seams like happy pals.
A snap here, a clip there,
Creating outfits that make us stare.

A zipper dreams of opening wide,
While cape clasps wish for a daring ride.
Each little piece has hopes to chase,
In a bustling wardrobe, they find their place.

A button popped off from a wild night,
It wishes to party till morning light.
The hook and eye share secret wishes,
For dashing looks and yummy dishes.

So let's toast to the tiny crew,
For small fastenings who see us through.
With laughter and flair, we prance and dance,
In this fabric revolution, let's all take a chance!

A Pinch of Providence

In the sewing box, fate's wild card,
A friendly button is never too hard.
It helps to patch up rips and tears,
With a pinch of luck and little cares.

Last night's mishap? A drunken dance,
One button popped; what a romance!
It rolled away with a cheeky grin,
Sewing tales of where it had been.

From grandma's dress to a funky shirt,
Each piece holds memories, a little spurt.
And in this chaos, fun is found,
In every stitch, joy's tightly wound.

So let's embrace this merry fate,
A pinch of thread, don't hesitate.
With buttons and laughter, our stories unfold,
In this sewn-up world, we're brave and bold.

The Cord of Connection

In a world where socks go stray,
And breakfast drinks spill away,
A tethered laugh makes us grin,
Connecting hearts, let fun begin.

With every tug, a giggle grows,
Tangled tales that no one knows,
A lopsided dance, we shuffle along,
In mischief's shout, we all belong.

Invisible threads in life we tie,
Pull them tight, watch spirits fly,
A twist and turn, we laugh and cheer,
For these wild bonds, we hold so dear.

Every slip and every fall,
Links our stories, one and all,
So grab a friend, let silly reign,
In this tapestry, there's no disdain.

Weaves of Whimsy

In a fabric shop of dreams so bright,
Patterns dancing, what a sight,
A snip, a snare, what will unfold?
Nonsense tales in threads of gold.

With every stitch, a chuckle new,
Creating mayhem, just for you,
Quirky shapes come out to play,
Spinning chaos, hip-hip-hooray!

A patchwork quilt of oddity,
Sewn with joy and comedy,
Twisted fibers twirl and tease,
In this merry mess, we're sure to please.

Through weaves of laughter, let's collide,
In a world where whimsy's our guide,
Each thread a whisper, bold and spry,
Crafting silliness that's never shy.

The Matrix of Meaning

In a grid of giggles, secrets hide,
Connections form, side by side,
What's a quirk without a friend?
In this maze, let laughter blend.

Navigate through goofy schemes,
As reason bows to wildest dreams,
Chaotic paths seem right and wrong,
Yet every twist, it feels like song.

Link by link, we parse it out,
Giggling 'til we scream and shout,
In this puzzle, we find delight,
As nonsense dances through the night.

Witty signs that lead us near,
A maze of clowns, we show no fear,
In tangled thoughts that spark the play,
Here's where the fun will always stay.

The Embrace of Expectations

In the cradle of quirks we nest,
Where hopes and laughter are the best,
Two left feet and mismatched shoes,
In awkward grace, we can't refuse.

Around the corner, plans may sway,
Expect the weird to come our way,
With open arms, we laugh and spin,
For every blunder is a win.

We gather 'round the table, cheer,
Serving chaos with a side of beer,
Holding tight to dreams unmet,
We toast to life's most funny debt.

Amidst the quirk, we find our bliss,
In joyous hugs, there's no abyss,
With every stumble, we rise anew,
In this embrace, we laugh right through.

The Stitched Mosaic

In a patchwork quilt a cat did hide,
With mismatched squares, it took a ride.
Each thread a tale from days gone by,
Stitches dance like marionettes, oh my!

A button's pop sends crumbs like rain,
Chasing crumbs on a wild train.
It trips and flips with every turn,
In this silly seam, we laugh and yearn.

Who knew a thread could pull this way?
We're tangled up in games we play.
With each new loop, a giggle grows,
A merry dance in fabric shows!

So let's embrace the quilt of fate,
With silly stumbles that just can't wait.
In every stitch, a chuckle lies,
We're sewn together, oh what a surprise!

Twists in Time

A clock once ticked in a wobbly way,
Telling tales of a silly day.
It promised noon when it was one,
And made us all chase a runaway sun!

With a twist of fate, we lost the time,
As ants wore hats and danced in line.
We laughed so hard, we struck a pose,
In a wacky world where laughter grows.

The seconds slipped like jellybeans,
In a wild parade of silly scenes.
We raced with clocks, they spun in mirth,
In this strange land, we found our worth!

So let us turn the dial of glee,
In a nonsensical tapestry.
With every tick, the fun transcends,
A twist in time that never ends!

Fated Fastenings

A jacket stuck on a doorknob tight,
Pulled my friend in with all its might.
"Help!" he yelled with a grin so wide,
"I'm fashionably late, just along for the ride!"

Zippers crisscrossed like lovers' lace,
In a wardrobe war, oh what a chase!
With every tug, we burst with glee,
In a closet brawl of destiny.

Fasten up your shoes, here comes the laugh,
As socks take flight on a comedic path.
With every snap and playful twist,
We found new joys that can't be missed!

So let's embrace our tangled attire,
With laughter building, getting higher.
In fated fastenings we thrive,
With silly moments, we come alive!

Embroidered Encounters

Two squirrels met with a thread in hand,
Sewing dreams like a funny band.
They stitched a park into a hat,
With nuts and seeds where laughter sat!

Each patch a tale that made us grin,
Of playful chaos where friends begin.
With coats of color, they drew the scenes,
In a funny world of jesting fiends.

One squirrel slipped on a fabric wave,
"Hold on tight!" his buddy gave.
They tumbled down, a fluffy ball,
What a delight, a giggle for all!

So gather round for the charm they weave,
In embroidered laughter, we believe.
With every thread that we intertwine,
Joy blossoms forth like cherry wine!

The Toggle of Tomorrow

In the realm of switches bright,
I toggle left, I toggle right.
A click, a clack, what could it be?
A dance party or a cat on a tree?

Giggles echo in the air,
As I weave through this wacky fair.
One press turns the sun to rain,
Next press, I'm upside down on a train!

What a mess this toggle makes,
Spaghetti monsters and silly flakes.
But lost in laughs and pure delight,
I'll dance 'til dawn, with all my might!

So here's to switches, life's silly game,
Tomorrow's toggle won't be the same.
But up and down, I'll join the fun,
In this wild, wobbly world, I'll run!

Weaves of Wanderlust

Tangled threads on a sunny day,
I pull one loose, and oh! It's gay!
A laughter stitch that starts to twine,
Around my thoughts, oh what a line!

With every tug, a tale unfolds,
A pirate ship or a castle bold.
Mismatched socks and shoes that squeak,
My wardrobe's chaos makes me peak!

Wanderlust in every weave,
A patchwork quilt I can believe.
Each pull a journey, far and wide,
With knotted dreams on the wild side!

So spin the yarn and watch it flow,
Each twist of fate, a merry show.
Weaves of whimsy, travel where?
In my crazy closet, anywhere!

The Click of Change

A little click, oh what a sound,
Transforming lives all around!
With every tap, a giggle sparks,
Like a chicken crossing, leaving marks!

I clicked for breakfast, now it's lunch,
A wild buffet that packs a punch.
A dinner date with fork and knife,
And suddenly, I'm a squirrel with a life!

Click my shoes and I can fly,
Bouncing high, oh me, oh my!
Hiccups make me whirl and twirl,
In this chaotic, joyful whirl!

So here I click, with glee and cheer,
Changing moments, far and near.
One click closer to the strange and odd,
In this merry world, oh how I nod!

Hooks of Hope

In the closet of my wacky dreams,
Hang hooks of hope, where laughter beams.
One pulls a joke, another a dance,
While the rubber chicken takes its chance!

With every hook, a story glares,
A silly outfit or wild hair flares.
One is pink, and one's bright blue,
Together they giggle, a colorful crew!

Unraveled threads of joy and cheer,
Hooks swing low, but never fear.
Each pull a promise, a grin in sight,
A path to giggles, oh what delight!

So hang your hooks, my jolly mates,
Let every laugh unlock great fates.
In this world of whimsy and joy,
Every twist and turn, oh boy, oh boy!

The Loom of Life

In a world where socks go astray,
And your lunch goes missing, hey!
A twist of fate may just unfold,
As you wear mismatched socks, bold!

The cat steals yarn, what a mess!
Tangles turn into a dress!
A trip on air, a hop, a skip,
Life's joys are found in each little quip!

So grab your thread with playful cheer,
Turn life's mishaps into beer!
For every loop, a giggle flies,
In the loom of life, we wear our ties!

The Weave of Whimsy

In the fabric of our silly days,
Life's little quirks get tangled in play.
A donut that rolls right off the plate,
Who knew dessert could tempt such fate?

Woven dreams of zany cheer,
Like a clown jogging in flip-flops near!
A surprise around every twist,
Join the dance—don't you dare resist!

With each thread a laugh we find,
Silly moments, so unrefined.
In the loom of whimsy, come and see,
Every twist—the fun sets you free!

Threads of Fate

Life is a tapestry hanging high,
With threads that stick and sometimes fly.
When fortune's tapestry has a hole,
Just patch it up with a savory roll!

A stitch gone wrong, oh what a sight,
A hat sewn crooked feels just right!
You'll find your way through mismatched seams,
As laughter bursts forth in zany dreams!

Embrace the fray, don't be too straight,
In this quirky weave, we celebrate!
So thread your fate with a dash of glee,
And watch the knots unravel, whee!

Stitches of Tomorrow

Tomorrow's stitches are cut from today,
With threads of humor that lead the way.
A collar that's sewn with silly fluff,
Makes your wardrobe pop—never tough!

The patterns whirl in a colorful dance,
As silly surprises give life a chance.
That coffee spill, it paints the scene,
Each stitch a burst, like laughter, keen!

So gather your needles, don't you pout,
For life's sweet fabric, we're all about!
Stitch a future bright and bold,
With humor as our secret gold!

The Ties that Bind

In a world of threads and seams,
We tie our fates with silly dreams.
A shoelace tangle, fate's design,
Oh look, I've tripped! It's quite divine!

Next time I'll wear my fluffy socks,
Avoid the trips, the midnight knocks.
A wardrobe choice that's quite absurd,
Who knew my shirt would speak a word?

It winked at me, oh what a sight!
Reminded me to dance tonight.
With colors bright and patterns wild,
Life's like a quirky, laughing child.

So here's to ties that make us grin,
So awkward, yet we still can win!
Let's dance on strings, be brave, be bold,
Embrace the laugh, let stories unfold!

Spheres of Significance

Life's a ball, a funny game,
Each twist and turn, never the same.
Round and round we bounce about,
With every slip, we laugh and shout!

I rolled through town, a sight to see,
Chasing cats, and spilled my tea.
The folks just laughed, what a delight,
A giggle fest beneath the night!

In spheres of fate, oh what a mess!
I planned so well, but who could guess?
My calendar's a riddle unsolved,
Yet here's my joy, completely evolved!

Juggling life like a clown with glee,
Every oops becomes a spree.
So join the fun, don't run or hide,
We'll dance in circles, side by side!

Hooks of Happenstance

Once I hooked my coat on a peg,
And ended up dancing like a beg.
Twisting round in a knotty pose,
Life's little gags, how it overflows!

Every chance encounter's a joy,
A hiccup here, a silly ploy.
Met a llama at the grocery store,
It winked at me, I fell to the floor!

Each hook feels like a punchline told,
A twist in fate, or so I'm sold.
They pull me in, make me a fool,
But laughter's magic; it's my rule!

So here's to snares that make us laugh,
A playful jest, a quirky path.
In life's big web, we dance and sway,
Hooked on joy; hip-hip-hooray!

The Patchwork of Possibilities

Stitching together a dreamy quilt,
With patches of laughter, nonsense spilled.
Each square a story, colorful flair,
Funky patterns dancing in the air!

I saw a cat, a pirate too,
In a jigsaw piece, how about you?
Gave it a wink, oh what a sight,
We laughed so hard, it felt just right!

The fabric of fate is a cozy weave,
With every twist, a chance to believe.
I'll sew a patch of silly love,
A little mischief from above!

So gather round, let's craft our dreams,
In stitches of folly, or so it seems.
With threads of fun, we'll boldly roam,
In this patchwork quilt, we find our home!

The Clutch of Continuity

In pockets deep, we stash our dreams,
Where loose change jingles and laughter beams.
A sock's a friend when missing a shoe,
In this crazy game, we're all in a zoo.

What if today a shirt spoke back?
Would it sass or pluck? Would it be on track?
The belt holds tight, but pants have a say,
In this wardrobe dance, we frolic and sway.

Zippers giggle, buttons pop free,
With seams that whisper sweet mystery.
In this fashion show of fate's own whim,
Even ties can get loose and dance on a whim.

So let's embrace with a wink and a jig,
Life's outfit is quirky, not just a fig.
For every outfit's tale has a twist to unveil,
In this fabric of joy, let's set sail!

Collars of Coincidence

A hat tipped low in a sunny embrace,
Declared the ruler of the park's wide space.
Socks without pairs, they scheme on the floor,
As we step out, they conspire for more.

The napkin decided to join the show,
With stains of spaghetti, it steals the glow.
Who wore it best? The shirt or the tie?
An infinite debate as we venture awry.

With pockets that giggle and shoes that sing,
What strange outfits will tomorrow bring?
Berets and scarves, oh what a blend,
In this circus of clothing, there's no end!

So cheers to the wardrobes that shout and delight,
In this fabric of chaos, we twirl with pure sight.
Every layer a chuckle, every seam a grin,
In the theater of clothing, let the fun begin!

The Nest of Necessity

In closets where socks go to hide and play,
The oddest of pairings brighten the day.
A dishcloth may start a hilarious feud,
While forks and spoons share food with rude attitude.

Under the bed, dust bunnies do tango,
Joining the fun with a chuckle and dango.
They nudge the cat, who does not approve,
In this quirky nest, there's always a groove.

The silverware clinks, it's having a ball,
As teaspoons plot mischief, plotting for all.
With whispers of crumbs hidden behind,
In this wild kitchen, hilarity's blind.

So gather your goodies, let laughter abound,
In homes where the silly is always profound.
With joy in each corner, let's paint the day bright,
In the nest of necessity, we dance into the night!

The Loop of Life's Lessons

Around we go in this funnel of fate,
With mismatched shoes feeling pretty great.
A tie caught a lift on a friend's briefcase,
In this comical race, of time and space.

Life's loops spin swiftly, like a skirt in the air,
Where the left sock insists it's a fashion affair.
Meanwhile, the sweater suggests a nice pout,
In this stitching of fate, we laugh and shout.

Each error's a style, each misstep a win,
While plaid fights stripes, let's all join in!
With patches of laughter sewn into seams,
Our wardrobe's a canvas for our wild dreams.

So twirl through the cycles, let silliness reign,
In this endless loop of delightful disdain.
For life is a fabric woven in cheer,
In the loop of our lessons, let's dance without fear!

Intersections of Intent

A popped button rolled away,
Chasing dreams that choose to stray.
It danced with fate on busy streets,
While folks just stared, their laughter greets.

A squirrel picked up the shiny round,
It thought it found a treasure found.
But alas, it rolled into a shoe,
To squeaky steps, its journey flew.

In the end, the button sighed,
As it joined the lone sock's ride.
Oh, what a twist in life's own game,
Where whimsy reigns and none feel shame!

So when you lose a round delight,
Embrace the twist, the funny fight.
Intents may tangle, and that's just fine,
For laughter always draws the line.

The Loom of Life's Journey

In a buzzing loft where threads entwine,
A weaver hummed to whims divine.
She stitched the fabric of each day,
With giggles woven in the fray.

A fray became a dance with fate,
As mismatched patterns learned to mate.
The looms would jiggle, twitch, and shake,
Creating wonders, make no mistake!

Colors clashed in joyful glee,
A tapestry of chaos, see?
Each knot a story, twisted tight,
That made the tapestry so bright.

As hours pass in threads we spin,
Each laugh embeds a joyful grin.
Our journey's clumsy, that's okay,
For life's a quilt of fun and play.

The Seamstress of Serendipity

At her old shop, the seamstress twirled,
With mismatched fabrics, her magic swirled.
She stitched together tales so grand,
With threads of laughter crossing hand.

One day a chicken waddled in,
Seeking pants to win the win.
"Make me chic," it clucked with glee,
"A dapper look is key for me!"

She tossed some fabric, bright and bold,
With polka dots, oh what a fold!
In seconds flat, the bird was dressed,
Leaving townsfolk quite impressed.

Laughter echoed down the street,
As tiny feathers danced on feet.
The world is silly, can't you see?
For joy comes wearing quirky spree!

Points of Attachment

In a land where zippers had to shout,
A threadless creature roamed about.
"Can anyone help me find my mate?"
It cried aloud, "Oh, isn't fate!"

A little hook with a cheeky grin,
Swung from a coat, "Come join my kin!"
They met and laughed, such a random bind,
Life's little pleasures tangled, twined.

Together they danced on a loose string,
Finding joy in just about anything.
With each twist and turn, they found the way,
Laughing loudly throughout the day.

So if you're feeling lost, don't fret,
Strange connections, you won't regret.
Just look for the thread, or the cheeky hook,
Life's mishaps make the best storybook!

Seams of Significance

In a closet where shadows lurk,
A sock claims it's the king of work.
With mismatched flair, it struts about,
Proclaiming loudly, "Look at me, no doubt!"

A shirt winks slyly, its collar askew,
"I'm the life of the party, who knew?"
Meanwhile, a belt jokes with a shoe,
"Tighten up, pal, you've got nothing to do!"

Threads of Tomorrow's Quest

A thread plucked from a jacket seam,
Dreams of riches in a wild scheme.
It dives on a journey through laundry's might,
Chasing the washing machine's spinning light.

It twists with excitement, takes a wild leap,
Dodging lint monsters, then takes a peep.
"I'll weave through worlds, oh what a thrill!"
Onward it goes, with a laugh and a chill.

The Harness of Happenstance

A belt took a stroll through the park one day,
Clipped on to fate without much to say.
"I hold up the pants, but I've got dreams too,"
"Perhaps I could play in this wild debut!"

It turned to the shoes with a wink of delight,
"Let's march through the grass, make our futures bright!"

They giggled and danced, oh what fun they had,
While reminding themselves, they were not quite a fad.

The Clip of Fate's Dance

In a drawer where chaos reigns supreme,
Clips wiggle and giggle, living the dream.
One clip flips, saying, "I'll hold the place!"
"But I'll steal the show," says a scrunchie with grace.

Together they twirl in a wild ballet,
Making mischief in a magical way.
"Hook onto this, let's snatch our chance,
For life's too short for a boring dance!"

Fastening a New Path

In a world where zippers squeak,
And shoelaces tie in a peak,
I found a clip that claimed to steer,
My path ahead, quite sincere.

With every snap, a new chance bound,
A dance of fate in a jolly round,
I tripped on smiles, but who would ask?
In jest, I wore my life's great mask.

The buckles laughed, the clips complied,
As I donned hats that reclined,
With each new loop my foes would flee,
Life's tangled mess became my glee.

So here I stand, embracing the flair,
Of wit and whimsy in the air,
Each twist and turn, a laugh parade,
My quirky fate, in charm arrayed.

The Click of Convergence

A click of fate, I heard it sound,
As mismatched socks danced round and round,
In every gap, a silly fit,
Converging dreams, we laughed a bit.

From forks in paths to tangled leaves,
Mismatched buttons weave few reprieves,
But with each poke, a grin does lay,
As we stumble, laugh, and sway.

The zippers lifted spirits high,
Like cheerful kites that touched the sky,
Intertwined paths, a funny twist,
Who knew that paths could be such bliss?

So let's embrace this comical ride,
With every click, we'll laugh and slide,
The universe in stitches here,
Converging joy, our hearts sincere.

Interlaced Journeys

Two shoelaces crossed in a race,
A twisted fate, a silly face,
We tangletangled, lost our stride,
Each twist of thread, a bumpy ride.

A clasp then joined in raucous cheer,
We wove new routes far and near,
With every step, a laugh would ring,
As fuzz and frays would start to sing.

The journey's charm, a patchwork quilt,
With mismatched pieces deftly built,
In every loop, a story spun,
To dance through life and have some fun.

So here we go, a motley crew,
With threads of laughter, bright and new,
Interlaced and wild, yet all in sync,
In every stitch, we stop to think.

Threads of Tomorrow

When yesterday's threads begin to fray,
I take today's twists to lead the way,
A colorful strand pulls me up tight,
To seek the laughter, all day and night.

With every knot, we grumble and grin,
Each snag a lesson, a twirl within,
The fabric of life, a tangled spree,
Every thread, a chance to be free.

The weaver cackles, her loom's abuzz,
As I juggle fortunes, like tops that fuzz,
In every stitch, a hope does glimmer,
For threads of tomorrow, our laughter grows shimmer.

So here's to the crafts and stitches we make,
In a patchwork world, we laugh, quake,
With every thread, our spirits soar,
In this wacky life, there's always more!

Stitching Threads of Fate

In the sewing room, chaos reigns,
Fabric monsters dance with chains.
A thread gets stuck, oh what a mess,
Sewing skills put to the test.

The cat swipes at shiny pins,
While I'm just hoping it begins.
A patchwork life of laughs and quirks,
Stitches made with giggles and smirks.

Every tiny hole brings glee,
A mishap loved, oh can't you see?
Lopsided seams, my heart skips a beat,
With every stitch, life's pretty neat.

So if your fabric starts to fray,
Just find your humor, don't dismay.
In threads untamed, we find our fate,
Laughing while we navigate!

The Closure of Choices

Fasten your seatbelts, it's that time!
To choose a stitch, oh what a climb!
Zigzag, straight, or maybe a curve,
These crafting paths make me swerve.

A button here or a snap right there,
Many options fill the air.
Will I go for plaid or polka dots?
Decisions, decisions, connecting the knots.

I reach for green, but it feels so wrong,
What shade of yellow sings my song?
The fabric shrugs as I sit in shock,
Swapping threads like a sock drawer clock.

With every clip, I'm unsure and bold,
The tales of fate yet to be told.
It's all a game, a playful dance,
In this patchwork world, it's my chance!

Fastened Futures

Dancing threads just weave my day,
Creating futures in a funny way.
A bright pink fabric, silly as can be,
Accidental outfits, that's the key!

Every button holds a little joke,
Like "Will it fit?" with every poke.
I stitch together bits of glee,
Crafting dreams with great esprit.

As I gather scraps and confetti,
The future's plump, but my wallet's petty.
What will I wear to the big parade?
I'll just use fabrics that aren't afraid!

A zip here, a snap just for fun,
In every misfit, I have won.
So let's sew tight and laugh a lot,
In our wacky futures, we hit the spot!

Threads Unraveled

Unraveling chaos, thread on the floor,
The cat thinks it's a fun little war.
Snagged on a hem, oh what a sight,
Every stitch is a brand new bite.

The fabric howls with every tweak,
As I attempt this daring technique.
Is it a dress or a comedy show?
Designed by fate in a dazzling glow.

A tool from the kitchen, a temporary fix,
Gotta think quick, oh what a mix!
A fork for a hem, who would have guessed?
In a world of wits, I'm truly blessed.

So let the seams hang loose and free,
With laughter echoing from the seams of me.
In every mishap, joy is revealed,
In threads unraveled, fate is sealed!

Knots of Possibility

Tangled threads in hands I hold,
Each twist can turn to stories bold.
A loop, a bend, a hopeful chart,
Each scribble can inspire the heart.

In every knot, a tale unfolds,
Some are bright, and others cold.
A dance of chance, a hearty laugh,
Life's messy tapestry, the best half.

With every pull, the laughter grows,
A circus act, as everyone knows.
Tying dreams with threads of cheer,
Who knew knots could bring such leer?

So grab your yarn and let it flow,
Knots of fate, put on a show!
Make a scarf or make a mess,
At least we'll find some silliness!

The Sequence of Serendipity

In numbers strange, I find my way,
A shuffle dance, come out and play.
Each step a giggle, a cosmic jest,
Unexpected turns, life's little test.

Two and three, then something new,
A funny hop, both me and you.
Math can be a prankster's game,
Add a laugh, it's never the same.

Like pizza slices, life's a pie,
Cut it funny, don't be shy.
Serendipity's quirky trance,
Join the dance, give fate a chance!

So jot it down, your jumbled path,
Add some giggles, subtract the wrath.
The sequence moves, go grab your hat,
With laughter locked in chic format!

Latchkeys to Life

In pockets deep, the keys I find,
To doors of joy and tales entwined.
Some fit snug, while others jiggle,
Unlocking laughter, oh what a giggle!

A rusty one opens up the sun,
While sparkly keys can bring the fun.
Each twist is a wink from fate's own face,
Unlocking secrets, a playful race.

Life's a vault, perplexing and grand,
With every turn, a funny strand.
Tap the clang or give it a knock,
Find that door, unlock the clock!

So grab your keys, don't hesitate,
Open those locks, step past the gate.
With laughter echoing, and dreams in tow,
Life's little treasures will start to flow!

The Pinwheel of Paths

Round and round, the colors spin,
Chasing breezes, where to begin?
Paths diverge in giggly bends,
Crafted by fate, where laughter sends.

With each puff, a new quest starts,
Like a child's play, it wins our hearts.
Let the wheeling take you high,
And watch life whirl, just let it fly!

Spin to the left, then spin to the right,
Every turn brings sheer delight.
A burst of fun, a whirling cheer,
Paths collide, "Hey buddy, come here!"

So chase that pinwheel, make it dance,
Silly moments are here by chance.
Life's a carnival, bright and bold,
Just hold on tight; let dreams unfold!

Choices Unraveled

In a world where choices dance,
One can trip and lose their pants.
A left turn leads to ice cream land,
While right takes you to a marching band.

Should I wear polka dots today?
Or stripes that shout, 'Hip-hip-hooray!'
The choices twirl, a dizzy sight,
Each step a giggle, pure delight.

A hat that squeaks, a tie with flair,
Will make the crowd stop and stare.
Mistakes can lead to joy anew,
Just laugh it off, a silly view.

From socks that clash to tops that spin,
Life's a game we laugh to win.
So button up with style, oh please,
Embrace the quirks, just smile with ease.

The Toggle of Time

A flick of fate within my hand,
Switched my tea to soda, bland.
I blinked and missed a silly cat,
Who danced like a chipmunk, imagine that!

An hour's passed, I lost my way,
Chasing clocks that run astray.
Tick-tock, tick-tock, what a fuss,
I turned my watch; it ticked on us!

Back to last week's fashion show,
Where I wore socks that stole the glow.
The toggle pulled, now look at me,
Past or present? Crazy glee!

In the twist and whir of time's parade,
Life's a stage where clowns are made.
So grab that switch, and don't you pout,
Let laughter lead, that's what it's about!

Hoops of Hope

Through hoops of fate, I danced today,
In oversized shoes, I swayed and swayed.
With each jump, laughter came around,
I tripped, then rolled upon the ground.

Oh, the tricks I tried to achieve,
A flip, a twist, then I did grieve.
The laughter echoed, bright and loud,
As I fell flat, a dancing clown!

With every bounce, a twist of chance,
I reveled in this silly dance.
Hoops of joy, a wobbly feat,
Each tumble said, "Get back on your feet!"

So leap through life with glee galore,
Embrace the joy, and always soar.
With hoops of bliss, we'll find a way,
Just laugh and cheer through every day.

The Fabric of Intention

In threads of luck, my plans unwind,
A tapestry of funny, blind.
I stitched a dream, but oh, you know,
I used a sock, now where'd it go?

With every pull, a story spins,
A patchy life with silly wins.
A blanket here, and a hat gone wild,
Crafting chaos, like a child.

The fabric laughs at every bend,
Weaving giggles that never end.
Mistakes that twirl like autumn leaves,
Each stitch, a tale the heart believes.

So sew your dreams with colors bright,
In a quilt of zany, pure delight.
For in this fabric, fun abounds,
With giggles echoing all around.

The Snap of Serendipity

In a room of mismatched socks,
A chance encounter, who would have thought?
A sudden snap, a joyful whizz,
A laughter shared, I must admit.

One sock spins, and then it dives,
Into the laundry's secret lair.
What follows next is pure surprise,
As objects dance without a care.

A button bounces, little did we know,
It lands on fate's own fashion show.
With every twist, a tale unwinds,
Of silly spats and joyful finds.

So here's to all the quirky runs,
To happy accidents and gleeful puns.
In the game of life, sometimes we find,
The funniest paths are purely blind.

Woven Whispers

In a closet where the secrets hum,
A tapestry of tales begun.
Threads of laughter, stitches of cheer,
Every loop tells a story here.

A fabric patch that's boldly shined,
Some colors clash, yet it's divine!
With each embrace, a giggle bursts,
In chambray dreams and polka dot firsts.

Snagged on a sneeze, a quilt took flight,
Sending feathers up into the night.
Who knew a sneeze could cause such joy?
Life's fabric twisted—oh boy, oh boy!

So let us weave our whims away,
In lively threads, let's choose to play.
For every flap and every twitch,
Laughing makes the world feel rich.

The Tactile Tapestry

A giant patch of fluff and fuzz,
Creating chaos, all because!
A thumbtack tumbles, a fumble made,
And suddenly, a parade is laid.

Here comes a felt that's dressed in glee,
Rolls with joy, just wait and see.
With every pull, a giggle sent,
What a time—oh, what a event!

The yarn in knots performs a dance,
As kittens tumble, not by chance.
A tug of war, with winks and grins,
Where chaos wins, and laughter spins.

Each thread a laughter, each stitch a joke,
In this woven land, we provoke.
Life's fabric, frazzled yet divine,
We laugh together, and all is fine.

Choices in Every Stitch

In a seamstress' shop, a choice to make,
Should I take monster or cupcake?
A button glows, all spruced in flair,
While glitter shouts, "I'm happy here!"

Each fabric whispers, soft and loud,
"Choose me now, stand tall and proud!"
Thread of joy or lace of dreams,
In playful chaos, laughter beams.

With scissors poised, and giggles near,
A fashion mishap? No need to fear!
For every cut and every flip,
Life's full of giggles; it's quite the trip.

So sew your dreams, in colors bright,
Twisted tales and pure delight.
Every stitch that you embark,
Unfolds a laugh, ignites a spark.

www.ingramcontent.com/pod-product-compliance
Lightning Source LLC
Chambersburg PA
CBHW070006300426
43661CB00141B/265